# The Ultimate
# Knockout
## Closing System

20 **Heavyweight** Techniques - Catapults Your
Customers to YES! Plus The Secret 5 Step
Formula - Overcomes Every Objection

## Rob Purfield

# The Ultimate Knockout Closing System

### 20 **Heavyweight** Techniques - Catapults Your Customers to YES! Plus The Secret 5 Step Formula - Overcomes Every Objection

## Rob Purfield

# The Ultimate Knockout Closing System

# Foreword

I t's a knockout!

My memories of this expression are in the northern accents of the inimitable Stuart Hall and Eddie Waring as they introduced and presented the UK version of the programme known universally as "Jeux Sans Frontieres".

A game where the focus was on overcoming obstacles to reach an intended goal - no surprise here we are again – with more proven ways to achieve our sales goals and more ways to play without boundaries and score more knockouts.

I've lost count...

Of the number of sales books read or sales skills audio programmes bought and studied in my 39 years in business. As a life-long learner (like you) I'm happy to consistently devour the success thoughts of others. Why? Some people have asked me. Simply because it shortcuts my journey to success. Why make simple mistakes when someone already has and is happy to share how to avoid them.

And here we are now...

Reading the experiences and ideas and methods of one of the 'Real People' – someone who's been there and done it; someone who also has that rare ability – the ability to share their ideas with others – Rob Purfield.

You have in your hand...

An essential guide for any salesperson, entrepreneur or business owner – the key ways; the 20 key ways to get more business.

These days you and I hear people expounding the idea that 'closing sales' is no longer necessary. Consultative selling they preach avoids the need to 'ask for the order'. What complete and utter rubbish!

The true professional – helps their clients to experience the benefits of their products and services – and doesn't leave to chance the possibility of a business relationship good for both parties.

Why is it...

Some people haven't closed as many sales as they'd like to have closed – over the years? My research indicates 4 main reasons. First – they lack belief in what they're selling. Second – they are scared of rejection. Third – they don't know the words to use. Fourth – they haven't practiced the words.

Reason number 'one' they must get over on their own. Reasons 2-4 are solved – right here, right now in Rob Purfield's user-friendly '*Ultimate Knockout Closing System*'.

I wish I'd had this when I started.

*Peter*

Peter Thomson
www.PeterThomson.com

# Contents

**PART 2: Bonus Section**
**The Secret 5-Step formula...How to Overcome Every**

# How To Use This Book

This book is not necessarily designed to be read in a linear way, from front to back.

There is no storyline to lead you from one chapter to the next, the book is designed as a compendium of techniques, which you can build into a bespoke closing system to fit your sales process, a system that is proven and will increase your success when persuading others.

At the end of each explanation you will find a section called "Seconds out" - this is where you are on your own, and you can write down when and where you can build that close into your sales pitch. Each one starts with the phrase, "I can use this when I..."

Studying champion salespeople, one of the first things I noticed was that they kept a journal of all the sales pitches they make (even in high volume sales pitch arenas like Car sales, and Account reps making 5-6 customer visits per day), and fine tune their approach each time to improve their results, and that's because the old maxim of 'you can't manage if you can't measure' is as true here as anywhere. So this book has been written to help you do just that.

Of course it would be helpful for you to look through the contents of the book and at least flick through each technique and become familiar with what it is and how it works, remember these are not just for selling they will work in every aspect of your life where you are trying to persuade others (even the kids!) so take the time to try a few out as often as possible. The reason I suggest you try them is to get used to using them as they may not work first time out and, if we are not prepared to fail once in a while we will never accomplish anything new. Think about when you were a baby, if you had given up trying to walk after a few attempts then you would be slightly inconvenienced now!

Another good analogy is teaching the kids to ride a bike (or learning to ride a bike if you haven't had the pleasure of teaching kids yet) – you don't take them out on to a busy dual carriageway and send them on their way with best wishes. What you do is find somewhere safe and allow them to fail, support them, pick them up, dust them down and get them back on the bike to try again.

The same is true here, don't go into your biggest, most important pitch and try something untested! Find some safe places to use and practice theses techniques so you become comfortable with them and can blend them into your everyday vocabulary, see which ones work best for you and start using them regularly, then gradually add a new one until you have the whole system.

Of course if you do try them and they don't work, it doesn't mean they don't work (because they all do) it means you didn't do it too well! (If you have ever had a golf lesson you will know the feeling of improvement whilst with the Professional, only to fall back into bad habits after the lesson... the information from the Professional was valid, it is your execution of the techniques that is lacking.)

Review your pitch, look at your timing, get a feel for what the customer said and your response, and think about which technique you chose and how you delivered it, plus how you think it resonated with the customer.

Good Luck and Good Selling!

Also look out for the supporting DVD and CD Audio programmes that are available at www.RobPurfield.co.uk

# Introduction

Before we start, you need to consider this question - can you handle an extra £50,000 per year?

£50,000 per year was the immediate impact this closing system had on my earnings.

I have had many successes, and of course failures, as a salesperson during my career. I'm pleased to say that the successes now far outweigh the failures, both in terms of volume and value, and I put much of this down to learning how to use the 'Ultimate Knockout Closing System'

Learning how to put together a closing system that is effective in any sales situation has now catapulted my earnings way beyond my wildest dreams from the young man who first entered the sales profession all those years ago.

Key to this learning was the acceptance of failure and persistence. Indeed, I'm always amused when I meet salespeople who tell me they have closing ratio of 80% or more – my simple answer "you don't talk to enough people."

One of the biggest secrets to being successful at selling is to keep talking to more people and accepting that many will say no, in fact if you have more people saying yes than saying no to you, then quite simply - you need to talk to more people.

Persistence then is one key to becoming successful in sales. Unfortunately, persistence alone will only make you annoying and not necessarily more successful. However, persistence, together with excellent technique will make you a champion salesperson.

I feel fortunate, that in my career as a Salesperson, and as a Sales Trainer I've had the privilege to work with and study some of the world's top salespeople.

The overriding formula to success for the world's top salespeople is quite simply; persistence plus technique. Whilst I am not in a position to provide you with persistence, I have written this book to share with you a closing system which I have honed and polished over many years.

But, before we go any further, I must congratulate you. Because you are in the minority! Just by reading this book you are demonstrating the mindset of a future Champion of Sales.

This is because, when I ask average salespeople if they have read some sort of book in the last 12 months, on improving their ability to influence and persuade, or on sales technique, or body language the answer is surprisingly few. But the best people I have worked with and studied have themselves taken the time to study and assimilate the habits and techniques of other great salespeople. (Some organisations even buy their sales teams books and audio programmes to study!)

Sometimes people say to me that their own sales process is different or that things that work for one customer will not work for every customer, and to be fair they have a point – all be it a very small one.

These persuasion techniques work on everyone, from your kids, to your partner or significant other, right up to the highest echelons and boardrooms of industry and commerce.

The reason is simple – they are based on everyday language that people use all the time, but because we don't do it consciously we often use the right technique at the wrong time.

Of all the things that I get asked, how to close the sale would seem to be the most common.

# Introduction

My first foray into the world of sales was as a self-employed, commission only, double glazing salesman, and I can well remember the feeling in every sales pitch that something seemed to be missing. The other guys in the team seemed to be "closing out" their pitch and getting sales and earning money, when all I seemed to be doing was having nice conversations with people, showing them my samples!

I was curious as to what they were doing differently to me, so I canvassed their opinion. Their advice was quite simple, it was *"that I needed to learn some closing questions"* and of course they were only too ready to help.

Unfortunately, it seemed to me that they were talking about asking some 'fantastic' question at the end of the sales pitch which miraculously made the customer say yes! Furthermore, from my perspective - these "closing" questions seemed to be really obvious and I was afraid the customer would spot them and then laugh me off the premises for my clumsy attempt at 'getting' their business.

Needless to say, whilst I had limited success in my career as a double glazing salesman I didn't earn the kind of money I felt my talents deserved.

With the benefit of hindsight, there was nothing wrong with my desire, or my persistence, and this state of affairs was clearly due to my lack of technical expertise when it came to developing a successful sales pitch, and my lack of knowledge on how to get people to say yes!

It was some years later when I was fortunate enough to sit in on a sales course entitled "The Road to Excellence" where I first learned to develop a system of closing that began at the start of my relationship with a customer, and continued right the way through the sales process and actually resulted in people asking me for the business! This was in contrast to my double glazing colleagues having to think of some convoluted question at the end of the sales pitch.

That was the start of a truly remarkable journey for me, and my sales career started to really take off, closing more deals and also achieving higher order values. To date I think I have sold over £20 million worth of training and consultancy programmes to some of the biggest companies in the world.

This system of closing is proven and has been fantastically successful for me during the subsequent 20 years I've enjoyed in the sales arena, as a Sales Professional, and as a Sales Trainer and Consultant, and latterly as a Behavioural Psychologist.

This amazing closing system has enabled me to sell contracts to major organisations of £2 million each , when early in my sales career I couldn't close a contract for double glazing at £200.

Set out in this book is the "Ultimate Knockout Closing System" which identifies 20 key techniques for you to use when talking to customers. The magic is in the combination of the techniques and specialist language patterns which you can apply in every conversation you have with the customer.

Learning to close the sale is probably the number one skill every salesperson needs, and understanding the subtle, and the not so subtle questions you can ask customers, and learning to appreciate the timing of when to ask these questions will have a remarkable impact on your sales success.

The analogy used throughout the book is one of punching techniques for a boxer. World-class boxers are able to recognise the moves of their opponent and understand the timing of when to counter punch and how to use each particular punching technique, as well as putting them into combinations for real impact.

Similarly, you as a professional salesperson will also need to take these techniques, understand them, practice them and learn how to put them into combinations. And all the information you need to do that is right here in this book.

So I wish you every success, I hope you enjoy the book, and that you have as much fun as me in applying these amazing, proven techniques, GOOD LUCK and GOOD SELLING!

# 'About Closing'

Before we delve into the topic of closing, let's just take a moment to understand exactly what we mean by a "close"

Firstly, a close is not something that only happens at the end of a sale. This is a common mistake that beginners often make. Closing is something that you do throughout the entire sales process. In other words, you're always closing. You're constantly testing the waters. You should always know where you stand in the process, and moving the person in front of you to paying customer and closing the deal, should not be a magical mystery tour but a planned journey. In other words, if you are always testing the waters, you know before you get to the end that there is a potential problem, and you have the techniques to overcome that problem ... That's what this book is about.

Sometimes it will happen. You'll do everything you have been trained to do, get the customer nodding in agreement and you've presented as well as a champion can and you still have a problem. We go into that at length, don't worry. We cover it all, using real-life scenarios.

A close is not some magical statement to trick a customer into buying, or to change someone's mind who wasn't going to buy from you in the first place. No, a close is a question, which either confirms that the customer is ready to move on to the next stage of the process, or confirms in the mind of the customer that they are happy with whatever you have just said. It ultimately confirms that they are ready to buy.

J. Douglas Edwards, a famous American sales trainer, once summed it up with the phrase, "Questions are the answer."

Especially when it comes to selling! No one ever, "Told their way to a sale", but rather, champions do know how to, "Ask their way to a sale!"

And you should continually be asking questions. Indeed the golden rule of closing is;

- Always
- Be
- Closing

Here's an analogy for you, which I'll use a to illustrate my point. Closing techniques can be compared to punching techniques for a boxer. The more punches you have in your armoury and the more able you are to use them, the better boxer you will be.

Imagine if you can, what would happen if you only knew one punching technique. Say it's an uppercut. You throw your best punch and the opponent is still standing, looking at you. Having used the only method you have available, you are now in big trouble!

Continuing with this analogy, let's also consider what boxers do with their punches. They put them into combinations, and throw them one after the other. This keeps their opponent on the move and scores more points more often. It also keeps their opponents guessing, doesn't it?

Therefore, in selling we are looking for every opportunity we can to ask more questions; remembering of course that selling is about questioning your way to the finish line. It's also about changing up the routine. If you use a series of uppercuts, followed by a low blow to the abdomen, and the next time use the opposite, you now have two routines that work for you. Each situation is going to be as different as the customers you have to sell to. Some scenarios call for three of the closing techniques we'll cover, while others require the use of five.

One more thing to consider is that if you are really going to be a champion salesperson, you will stop making statements and start asking questions. Because, the only reason for making a statement is to pave the way for a question...isn't it?

On the topic of questions, there was one thing nobody taught me in sales training courses and it was this; **the best questions to ask are the ones I already know the answers to.**

That's right, everyone who has been trained in sales knows that they should ask a lot of questions. But, it was whilst I was studying the habits of the truly great salespeople that I realised they could easily anticipate the response they were going to get from the customer to each of their questions, because they not only planned their questions, they also gave some thought to the possible answers.

A good boxer will be able to anticipate an opponent's response to his attack; he can then plan his own defence and counter-attack accordingly. This takes experience but also confidence and sometimes even a little talking to yourself in front of the mirror. Practise makes perfect, doesn't it? Don't be embarrassed to try all of these out. Don't wait until you're with a customer, because that's the last place you should be "trying" anything for the first time. There is an expression, the more you sweat in the gym, the less you sweat in the ring.

Imagine, not just knowing what questions to ask and when, but also being able to predict how the customer will respond and then being one step ahead when planning your next question! Like the boxer, it's about anticipation. Being able to do this will, I assure you, make you a champion sales person, and all the information you need is here, in this book!

Once you have first learned, practised and then adopted these principles, you can and will increase your close rate, tremendously. Just remember, it's not a secret, it's a skill that you just haven't learned yet, and once you do, the world is your oyster... isn't it?

# 20 Heavyweight Techniques - Catapult Your Customers to Yes!

# The Direct Close
## Sometimes it's Worth The Risk

If you are new to selling, this can be one of the most difficult closes to master. Why, you wonder?

Asking direct questions is a risky business in the world of selling. Because, although you can anticipate the answer, (and you shouldn't really ask any question unless you can anticipate the answer) there is a danger that the answer will paint you into a corner.

That said, I am frequently amused how many sales trainers teach new salespeople that they should avoid asking direct questions. Much better, "they" say, to use open questions.

Open questions begin with:

- Who
- What
- Why
- When
- Where
- How
- And Which

However, open questions have their limitations too, the are excellent for eliciting information and your sales presentation should be peppered with them.

But, **DIRECT** questions – these are the ones that generally give you a yes or no answer and are the ones that get commitment.

Because the answer is either yes or no, they do fall into my category of being a question to which you already know the answer (it will either be yes or no).

Of course, the answer we all dread as salespeople is NO, but, if I have gotten to the stage where I believe I can ask the direct close "Can I have your business, please?" I must be comfortable that I have covered all the bases and therefore working on odds of at least 80/20 that the answer will be yes!

What happens in the event the customer says, "NO"?

Well, if you have done your job properly up to this point, you are entitled to say something along the lines of...

"Oh! I am sorry, what specifically is it that is stopping you from going ahead? What have I missed or not explained to you?"

Or perhaps

"That surprises me Mr Customer. May I be so bold as to ask you for some help?"

Wait for the affirmative (which is always the case)

"Can you coach me on what I would need to do to help YOU make a positive decision?"

Whatever comes up will be either "an objection" or "a condition".

An example of a condition would be something you need to do to get the sale (maybe a price concession or a specification amendment) and it would be up to your company and you whether you could meet that condition. If you can't, then you would have to resell the other benefits to justify to the customer not being able to match his full requirements.

An objection is usually something that you haven't explained properly or that the customer hasn't understood.

How to overcome objections is dealt with in the bonus section at the end of this book. (See page 95)

## So to Summarize:

A direct close is the same as a direct question, and is one that will usually force a yes or no answer.

It should only be used when you believe you have earned the right to use it and you have done a full professional sales presentation.

=== **Seconds Out...** ===

**The Direct Close** – A direct question asking for commitment.

I can use the Direct Close when I......

## The Alternative Close
### Always Give Them a Choice

For those of you who are veterans of linguistic techniques, you may recognise this technique under a different name, "The double bind".

But, whatever we call it, this is without doubt one of the most powerful closing techniques available and one that should be practised time and time again.

Writing the text for this book, I was reminded of a friend of mine who asked me for some help to improve the profitability of his Café Bar.

He told me that his biggest profit margin on the breakfast menu was on eggs, and that if he could improve his egg sales he would almost double his profit on each breakfast sold.

He also wanted to try selling eggs on different parts of his lunch/dinner menu.

My friend told me that he had tried everything to try and increase the sale of eggs, but with minimal effect.

When I looked at things more closely, I suggested he get rid of all the point-of-sale messages about eggs. For example, take the star bursts off the menu and off the counter and instead train his team to present meal options to his customers differently.

We then got the whole team together and showed them how to sell extra eggs.

And it amounted to this...

Whenever anyone asked for any kind of breakfast, the server would reach below the counter and produce two eggs and ask the question, "Would that be one egg or two?" Making sure we placed the emphasis on <u>two</u>.

But the biggest impact came on the sale of burgers. Once again, we asked servers, when they were asked for a burger, to reach below the counter, bring out two eggs and ask, "Would that be with one egg or two?"

Many people who had previously not considered an egg with their burger took one and others asked for two.

Eggs sales went through the roof and profits increased dramatically.

Now, many people ask me when and where <u>they</u> should use the alternative closing.

My answer is?..... Anywhere you can!

If someone calls your business to enquire about product details, always give them an alternative and sell up, For example, "Would you like details on the regular product or on the deluxe?" It should be automatic and part of your vocabulary.

Another way to utilise this technique is when making appointments, "When would be the best time for us to get together? Do you prefer the middle of this week or would you prefer later in the month?"

Let's take a look at a great example of using alternatives and creating what I call the "*alternative funnel;*"

Let's suppose that you are trying to make an appointment with a customer. Before we deal with the alternatives, let me introduce you to my 3 Golden Rules for getting appointments;

---

**Rule number 1:**

Distance the threat and by that I mean don't put too much pressure on by demanding to see them right away (even if that is your intention).

Give them some space and be open "Now or sometime later", is about as open as you can get for the customer, whilst the Now is really demanding!

**Rule number 2:**

Never ask for the appointment, just **assume** it will happen, by using a word like "When".
eg: "When would be the best time..." - not "can we?" or "will you"?

**Rule number 3:**

It's alternatives all the way down from here!

---

And of course the foundation for all of this is that you should never ask a question to which you don't already know the answer.

Got it? Great! Then let's try and build that funnel.

"Mr. Customer, when is the best time for us to get together? This week, or would you prefer some time next month?"

- We have distanced the threat covered (some time next month)
- We have been assumptive (when?)

- We have used an alternative (this week or next month)
- And we can anticipate the answer

Whatever the customer says, go for another alternative. Let's suppose they say "I'm busy this week...."

"Ok, next month? Would you prefer the beginning of the month or the end of the month?"

Whatever the answer is, use another alternative.

"The end of the month is fine. Would the third week or the fourth week be better for you?"

Again, whatever the answer use another alternative.

"Fabulous week four is great for me too. Shall we make it at the beginning of the week or the end of week?"

Use another alternative.

"No problem, Monday or Tuesday?"

And, another alternative.

"Monday then, morning or afternoon?"

There's one more!

"Monday afternoon is great with me. Shall we say just after lunch at two or later on nearer four?"

With that, confirm it!

"Monday the 27th, at four in the afternoon it is! Thank you."
And there we have it, the perfect funnel of alternative closing.

## So to summarize:

Alternative closing is a very powerful technique, which allows you to anticipate customer answers and to move the customer in your preferred direction.

## Seconds Out...

**The Alternative Close** – Always look to give your prospective customer a choice by using questions which end with an alternative.

I can use the Alternative Close when I......

# The Assumptive Close
## Always be Assumptive

Assumptive closing does exactly what it says on the tin. It's about tuning into the customer's verbal language as well as body language and assuming that he or she is ready to take the next step and move forward with the sale.

Assumptive selling requires you learn the art of using pre-suppositions. In other words, the way we phrase questions pre-supposes that something else must be true.

So, for example if we ask the customer:

"Where would you like to have the product delivered?" This pre-supposes that the customer will be buying your product and the only outstanding question is the delivery date. It's one way to move things to the closing stage.

Another way of using the assumptive sale can be by asking, "How will you be paying or that?" This again, pre-supposes that the sale will be made and the question remaining is the method of payment.

If you were selling a service you could ask, "When would you like to start?"

The psychology of the assumptive close is that you help the customer past the actual decision of whether to "buy or not buy" and to stay focussed on the "process" of buying. In this case, it's not about selling per se; it's about getting a customer in agreement with you.

In observing champion salespeople, I have noticed that they

always seem to have people buying from them rather than having to sell to them. The reason is that from the very first contact with the customer, they assume the sale and work on justifying the purchase to the customer, rather than focussing on persuading the customer that they want to buy their product or service.

This may be a subtle difference, but it is one that makes a massive difference in the way you deal with customers.

Therefore, my advice is always be assumptive in your approach to customers. This of course takes confidence that the customer wants to:

- Buy your product or service
- And likes you enough to buy it from *you*

We'll get into what happens when the customer wants the former and has an issue with the latter further on in the book.

But you have to assume that they want to buy your product or service, otherwise they wouldn't be talking to you in the first place....would they?

### So to summarize:

Always be assumptive in a way that pre-supposes moving on to the next step in the sale (or even the sale itself)

## Seconds Out...

**The Assumptive Close** – Never ask permission, always assume the positive....

I can use the Assumptive Close when I......

# The Decisional Close
## You Want a Commitment? Then I Want One, Too!

How many times have you had a customer ask you a question, which requires you to make a decision or a commitment?

For example, has any customer ever asked you a question that begins with the words:

"Could you get me some (discount?)"
"Would you be able to get delivery by the end of the month?"
"Will you throw in the accessories, as well?"

You get the idea. Well, these questions require that you make a decision and puts the customer in the driving seat, even if only temporarily.

I once designed a sales process for a client, based on the theory of, "Exchange Selling". The idea was that we found key points in the sales process where we were in a position to exchange things with the customer. Let me explain in more detail.

Let's say he or she wants special delivery terms on our latest product line.

My proposition would be this; we are legitimately in a position to exchange that commitment with a commitment from the customer.

We could respond with an answer such as, "If I can get you that delivery date, are you in a position to place a deposit immediately?" And it is this concept of exchange on which the Decisional Close works.

If the customer asks you to make a commitment, you can legitimately ask him or her to make one in return.

This does two things. It confirms serious intent to purchase and it shows her your intent to compromise, leaving her to feel she won something.

So, if the customer were to ask, "Could you get me some discount?" This is asking you for a commitment.

Trade that commitment by asking, "If I can, will you be in a position to place an order today?" (Assuming you are prepared to make the discount)

Going back to my earlier example of the customer's question, "Could you let me have delivery by the end of this week?"

Your answer could be, "If I can, will you be able to place your order today with a 50% deposit?"

Once again you have swapped or exchanged the requirement for you to make a commitment with a requirement for the customer to do the same.

## So to summarize:

Never, ever give anything away
Always, always trade it

## Seconds Out...

**The Decisional Close** – If the customer asks you for any kind of commitment, return the request.

I can use the Decisional Close when I......

# The Sharp Angle Close
## Are You Sure That's What You Want?

This one is very similar to the decisional close. The difference is subtle, but important. Previously, the customer was asking you for a commitment or a decision in the instance of the decisional close, the Sharp Angle is one you would use when the customer asks you a question about the product specification.

This in and of itself implies that the customer is warm. Any question, for example, asking for product information, indicates an interest, therefore, you need to be focussed on moving the situation forward.

For example, if you are selling beds, the customer might ask, "Does it come in King Size?"

If we were to use the decisional close technique, it would be a bit much if you were to respond, "If it does, will you buy one today?" In other words, it's too much, too soon.

It is much better to start the process of getting your customer into the "Yes mode" - remember every yes is another nail in the construction of your sales presentation.

So, a sharp angle close would work something like this:

The customer asks, "Does it come in king size?" Your answer would be, "Was it a king size you really wanted?"

Remember I believe that you should never ask a question unless you know the answer.

Well, the answer to this question is easy to anticipate.

The customer is hardly likely to say "No" if they have just asked the question are they? And, for the sake of argument, even if he or she did, it would still give you vital information in making your next statement.

But, in reality you can predict the answer to the question. And, if you think about it, this is one we use all the time without really realising it.

Here's an analogy Think back to the last time you telephoned your best friend and his or her partner answered the phone. You ask, "Hullo, is John there?"

What does she say? "Yes, he is out in the garden. Did you want to speak with him?"

You are not about to respond by saying, "No, it's ok I was just ringing to check on his whereabouts."

There in a nutshell, is using the sharp angle close. Just remember to use it when selling as well!

## So to summarize:

If a customer asks you for information, feed it back to him or her and get him or her to confirm what he or she wants and start the "yes" process.

It's important that you do not use it if he or she asks you for any kind of commitment or decision that would be an occasion to revert to using a Decisional Close.

**Seconds Out...**

**The Sharp Angle Close** – Is ideal for getting the customer into the 'yes' mode – "was it xyz you really wanted?"

I can use the Sharp Angle Close when I......

# The Trial Close
## Are We Cold, Warm or Sizzling?

Champion salespeople take every opportunity they can to test the temperature of the sale.

It is important that we know where the customer is in his own buying process; therefore we should be trying trial closes throughout the sales presentation.

A trial close is a vital skill in assessing what the customer is thinking. It requires you to be mindful of both verbal and non-verbal cues the customer is giving off.

Say for example you sell beds, and in your store is a customer looking at your top-of-the-range bed on display, which just happens to have a rather ornate brass bed head.

You could use a trial close such as:

"Would you like a bed head like that on your bed when you take delivery?"

There are three possible answers he can respond with:

"Yes, it looks really nice." This demonstrates that the customer is following your line of thought and you are on the right track.

You have potentially sold a bed *and* a bed head.

"No, I'm not sure that it would look right in our bedroom."

You certainly haven't sold a bed head but you may still have sold the bed! (It just needs a little more work.)

I guess there is also a third option, which might be.

"I like the bed but not the bed head."

This is a good signal that you will sell the bed, but don't hang around for the bed head sale.

Another example could be selling a service such as insurance.

Let's suppose that you are demonstrating a product for buildings insurance for your home, which includes contents insurance as well. You could say, "Is that the type of insurance you are looking for, buildings insurance with the contents included?"

Again there are a number of possible answers the customer can respond with:

"Yes, that sounds like the type of thing we are looking for."

You have potentially sold your buildings insurance and your contents offer is an attractive incentive.

"I'm not sure we need the contents, because we have contents insurance covered elsewhere."

You are not going to sell the contents, but you are still in the game for the buildings insurance. You see where this is going? Asking Trial Close questions usually lead you to the close. It may not mean that you'll get the whole kit and caboodle, but as Oprah Winfrey is so fond of saying, "You don't get what you don't ask for."

## So to summarize:

Trial closes give you the opportunity to "test the water" as you go through your sales presentation.

**The Trial Close** – Gentle questions that give the customer a safe place to say 'no' without jeopardising the sale.

I can use the Trial Close when I......

# The Puppy Dog Close
## Go on, Let Them Try it Out

This analogy is best demonstrated by taking you from your usual sales setting and placing you in a pet shop or a rescue shelter. You have a family in front of you and they cannot make up their mind about whether to take home the adorable puppy before them.

Having tried all your techniques but somehow you are unable to get them over the hump, you give them the option to take the puppy home for a trial period with the caveat that if they aren't fully  satisfied with her cuteness and ability to provide companionship, to bring her back in.

How many times do you think that would result in the dog coming back again? My guess? I've never heard it happening.

What can we learn from this scenario? Always, give the customer the opportunity to experience your product.

This message is often the reverse of the psychology most salespeople adopt. If you offer quality, excellent service at a competitive price, provide the customer with a physical experience, a demonstration, a test drive or some sort of trial and close the sale.

Experience tells me that most companies are happy for someone who is definitely going to buy from them to have a trial period, but are much more reluctant for potential customers who are undecided.

If you have ever bought a car from a car dealership, you may have experienced this. It can prove very difficult to get a test drive unless you are perceived to be a "buyer".

Frankly in my opinion, it is the people who are unsure what to buy who most need a test-drive more than anyone.

By contrast, many e-commerce and mail order companies allow you to keep their product for 30 days or more on a sale or return basis. Offering a full money back, no quibble offer, goes a long way to convincing the few that are uncertain.

Most people like to try on clothes before they buy them. When staring at ourselves in the mirror, we look very critically at both the outfit and ourselves, don't we? We want to know:

- Does the dress fit?
- What do the trousers look like on and how will they look with my favourite shirt?
- Do this outfit suit me?
- Does this skirt flatter me?
- Etc.

## So to summarize:

The puppy dog close is about offering your product/service and if necessary, with a no quibble return policy.

## Seconds Out...

**The Puppy Dog Close** – Let people try your product or service - set up a trial period, lend it to them... etc.

I can use the Puppy Dog Close when I......

# The Balance Sheet Close
## Creating a List of Positives to Get The Sale

This is ideal for the customer who just hems and haws. He can't decide what to do. You've given what you think is your best presentation, you've "pulled out all the stops" and even feel as though you could have "sold ice to an Eskimo". But this customer still has one foot twisted toward him, mouth curled up on one side, holding his right elbow with his left hand, while his closed fist rests comfortably against his face. Despite your best efforts, all he can say is, "I just don't know."

You think to yourself, "what is there not to know? I've presented the best alternatives to his problems and he still needs to contemplate his next move?"

These situations are the times when it's necessary to call on the great leaders of the world who have found themselves in similar predicaments ask yourself how they would have handled it. They certainly would not have let it go!

Because of the precariousness of the situation, the Balance Sheet Close has also been referred to as the "Duke of York", close, the "Winston Churchill" even the "Abraham Lincoln" close after these great leaders, who often found themselves in very sticky situations and who all learned how to resolve them effectively.

Before I explain how to use the balance sheet close, I need to stress the importance of presentation and the need for confidence in your delivery. Because if you lack confidence or are unable able to call upon it when needed and you present this close poorly, you may as well not have tried.

You will frequently hear me stress to all salespeople that I work with or coach, the importance of being mindful of every opportunity to make the customer feel comfortable; particularly if you want to engage them in the closing process. Nobody wants to feels as if they've been made to do something they were not comfortable doing.

When finding yourself in this predicament, my suggestion is that you display obvious empathy with the customer's position. You can achieve this by saying something along the lines of, "I can see that this is a big decision for you Mr. Customer, and I completely understand how you feel." This reminds me of what my Dad told me about Winston Churchill, when faced with a big decision would get a blank piece of paper and draw a line down the middle.

On the left side, he'd write, "YES" at the top and on the right, he'd write "NO". Under "Yes", he'd write all the reasons for going ahead. Equating this to a balance sheet close, yours could look like this:

| YES | NO |
|---|---|
| You did say that the **delivery date** was ok, didn't you?<br><br>You liked the fact that we could be **flexible** in our approach to the installation and work around your requirements. Is that correct?<br><br>If I heard you correctly, you also said that the **capacity** of the new machine was exactly what you are looking for, didn't you? | |

Now, you continue making every positive comment you can think of and list it on the Yes side of the page. (Aim for double figures here.) You read each one out loud as you write it and combine each point with a tie down close (see page 70).

When you have finished, you then turn the paper around for the customer to see, and say to him or her, "Obviously, I can't see any **negatives**, so why don't I let you fill those in?"

How many negatives do you think the customer will be able to think of? Experience tells me a maximum of two or three.

You can then conclude with, "Well, that looks fairly conclusive doesn't it? Shall we go ahead?" - Given that you will have listed many more positive reasons in favour of your product/service than the customer will have identified as negatives.

Remember, confidence and presentation are everything. I urge you to practice this one often in front of the mirror or with a colleague before attempting this with a customer.

## So to summarize:

This one needs practice and pen and paper. List all the positives, get the customer to confirm them, and then leave the negatives to them.

## Seconds Out...

**The Balance Sheet Close** – Confirm all the positives on your side and then let the customer come up with the negatives.

I can use the Balance Sheet Close when I......

# The Lost Sale close
## Concede First to Resurrect Later

This is a great technique to use when you get the response we all hate to hear, which is a flat out, "No" by your customer. In this case, there really is no reason not to use this one, as it only applies this instance.

How cool is that? There's a close to rescue the sale?

First of all, remember my rule about making customers comfortable? It's a rule that is always relevant, and always worth repeating. So, don't just launch into this one without bearing this mind. Also, this one is better implemented when you're face-to-face with the customer.

If we go back to our original analogy of closing being like punching techniques to a boxer, imagine how the customer feels after having been on the receiving end of your non-stop sales presentation. No doubt he or she is:

- Punch drunk
- Wobbly
- Unsure of him or herself

My advice is to relax him or her by saying something like:

"Ok, Ms. Customer, I can see that I have not managed to persuade you on this occasion to go ahead with our recommended solution."

At this point the customer is probably thinking that you are letting her off the hook. Next, stand up and extend your hand, which will serve to amplify this point. Whilst still holding hands, sit down again taking the customer with you.

Once you have your customer seated you can then say something along the lines of:

"Ms. Customer, I pride myself on my professionalism and whenever I am unsuccessful in outlining the benefit of our product or service I like to fully understand the reasons why. So, whilst we are together may I ask you one last question?"

The answer to this is likely to be yes, so follow up with:

"What one thing was it that I could have explained better to help persuade you to say yes?"

The answer to this will normally be around specification, price or timing. Once you've narrowed it down to one of these, this should be followed up with a final objection close

"And is that the only thing stopping us from going ahead?" If you can satisfy the outstanding query then you have just resurrected the sale.

If not, then at least you know that you tried your best.

The lost sale close takes a certain amount of courage, but it is definitely worth it, and above anything else is good fun to try.

## So to summarize:

Do not give in too easily, always try one more time, "what was the one thing I could have explained better...?"

53

**Seconds Out...**

**The Lost Sale Close** – Is when you are face to face and the customer says "*No!*"

I can use the Lost Sale Close when I......

# The Subject to Close
## Overcoming The Third-Party Objections

One of the most difficult situations for any salesperson to find him or herself in is the third-party objection.

In other words, after your presentation, the customer responds with any on of the following:

- I need to talk to my accountant
- I need to talk to my wife/husband
- I need to take it to the board

Now, once again, I must counsel you to have some empathy with the customer and make him or her feel comfortable. Frustrating as this may be, it's always advisable.

So, when faced with a third-party objection, the first thing you should say is:

"I fully understand, and if I were in your position I would want to talk with..... (fill in the blank with "my partner" "my accountant" etc).

"However, whilst we are both together may I ask you a question?"

The answer to this is always positive, as long as you have prefaced it with your expression of empathy first.

When he or she says, "Yes", your should follow-up with:

"If it were solely your decision would you be happy to go ahead?"

Because the customer has the safety of being able to blame some-one else, he or she will be more predisposed to answer positively.

Follow-up the close by stating that you will qualify the order form or contract with any on of the following:

- Subject to board approval
- Subject to partner's approval
- Subject to accountant's approval

Having done this, then ask the customer to approve the paper-work in the usual way, taking on board the lessons in the chapter on the very powerful Major/Minor close, which deals with shifting customer attention.

There we are, a very effective way of dealing with the response, "I want to think about it" that addresses the customer's concerns and still gets the sale closed.

## So to summarize:

When the customer offers a third party as an excuse to say no, always try to close them, and put the other party to one side with the "Subject to....." close.

## Seconds Out...

**The Subject to Close** – Is perfect when the customer says "*I need to talk to my....*" (third party.)

I can use the Subject to Close when I......

# The Major/Minor Close
## You Get More of What You Focus on

This is a lovely little close, which I have noticed all champion salespeople use in every sales presentation.

The purpose of this close is to lessen the impact of actually asking the customer to sign the order form. The golden rule, of course, is, "Never ask anyone to sign anything."

Why? Because, we have all been taught that we should take third party advice before we sign on the dotted line. It's much better to ask people to "ok" things or show their approval.

One car salesperson I met used to say, "Mr. Customer, I have been a big fan of yours for the last twenty minutes. Can I have your autograph here, please?" It may sound cheesy, but as soon as you ask the question, "Can you please sign here?" Customers can get noticeably nervous, regardless how often or how in depth you've explained the terms and met their objections. But, whatever you use, the Major/Minor close will help you to get the customer to sign.

Here's how it works. As you ask the customer to approve the paperwork, you take your pen out of your pocket; offer it to the customer and say, "Would you like to use my pen or yours?"

This diverts the customer's conscious attention away from signing the order or contract and focuses him or her on which pen to use.

One small point to bear in mind, which can make this even more powerful, is to ensure you always have a nice pen. It's a fact that people do like to write with nice pens.

In fact, this will add the customer's diverted attention as she is now mesmerised with your pen. She is certainly under no stress.

The major minor close would be, "Your pen or mine?" :)

## So to summarize:

Use the choice of implement needed to sign the order form as a diversion, than actually signing the order form.

=== **Seconds Out...** ===

**The Major/Minor Close** – Is a technique for asking the customer for commitment without using the words and focusing on a lesser choice (which pen to use).

I can use the Major/Minor Close when I......

# The Final Objection Close
## Don't Make Answering Objections a Habit

This close is designed to save you a lot of stress and hard work.

Often when observing salespeople, I notice them being led by the nose by the customer.

Remember that although you must be in a position to answer genuine objections, it is not your only role. You are not obliged to answer any and all objections. Identify the important ones that genuinely get in the way of the sale and focus your efforts on those.

However, the final objection close is a superb tool to isolate objections and ensure that the ones you receive are real.

When you receive a genuine objection from the customer, your response should be, "And, is that the only thing stopping you from going ahead?" It's a legitimate response to a legitimate concern on his part.

The customer has only two possible answers:

Yes, which means if you can satisfy the outstanding condition or objection then you have a sale.

No, which allows you to ask what else you need to explain in order to get a positive answer from the customer.

The final objection close is one you should use when faced with a genuine objection.

It's **not** be used when you've been able to answer a minor concern on the customer's mind. In other words, it's not to be used when he needs clarification about a point that you've already gone over, such as specification or price.

## So to summarize:

When the customer is requesting clarification, just answer. When there is a genuine concern, use the Final Objection close - "is that the only thing stopping us going ahead?"

---

### Seconds Out...

> **The Final Objection Close** –Is a great way to avoid answering objection after objection - *"is that the only thing stopping us from going ahead?"*

I can use the Final Objection Close when I......

# The Hope and Fear Close
## How to Create Urgency in Decision Making

This is ideal for those times when your organisation is staging a promotion of some kind. The promotion can apply to price, delivery date, product specification or anything. Without fail, there is always one customer who wants more than the promotion is offering.

Perhaps you've given in to his or her requests and made every concession available to him or her. But for whatever reason, she now wants the Sun and the Moon! In this situation, it's now necessary to roll up your sleeves and dig in. It's time to invoke the Hope and Fear close.

However, before attempting this, once again, I must emphasis the need to empathise with the customer and make sure that he or she feels comfortable. Nothing is ever achieved with your customer feeling anything but respected and understood.

That in mind, the first thing is to say something to diffuse the situation. You could use a phrase such as the following:

"Mr. Customer, I can see that you are having difficulty making a decision, and I understand how you must feel."

Having now relaxed the customer, we can then take the sale away from them. Seriously! We infer that if they continue to prevaricate then any benefit we have given him can be instantly taken away. Think about it. He is in a position where he feels in control.     Ultimately, it's about diffusing the situation, which is entirely within your control.

Your next move could be to say any of the following:

64

"In order to help you, I feel that I need to let you know that the 0% offer ends on Friday."

Alternatively, you can say:

"In order to secure you your desired delivery date, I do need a decision by the end of the day today."

The psychology behind removing any concession adds integrity to the initial offer, and puts positive pressure on the customer to decide in favour of buying. Once you get into a game of, "How about if I...?" This immediately puts the customer in a position of power and places you in the position of having to figure out how to climb out of the situation. The goal here is to take the power back, in a respectful and empathetic manner.

## So to summarize:

Be prepared to remove offers and concessions from the customer in order to face a decision.

## Seconds Out...

**The Hope and Fear Close** – Make sure all concessions are time bound.

I can use the Hope and Fear Close when I......

# The Reduce it to the Ridiculous Close
## Putting it Into Context

This is a superb technique for handling price objections. On a recent project we did with a motor dealership, the salespeople found this to be a particularly beneficial close.

The salesperson and the customer found themselves to be at an impasse and about £300 apart on the price.

Following the rule on making customers feel comfortable, he followed the process by saying:

"I fully understand your concerns with regard to the price difference, and with your permission I would like to examine them further. May I ask you how long you intend to keep your car?"

The customer answered "three years."

The salesperson continued, "So, over three years, the price difference would be the equivalent of how much per year?"

Leaving the customer to do the arithmetic, which is an important aspect of this scenario, the answer was of course £100 (£300/3 years).

The salesman followed up with, "May I ask you how often you use the car?"

The customer replied, "Every day."

Continuing the same theme the salesperson said, "So on a weekly basis that would equate to?"

Once again leaving the customer to do the arithmetic to get the answer, which was £2.

With one final push, the salesperson then asked what the equivalent would be on a daily basis.

The answer is obviously 30p. To complete the process the sales-person then said, "So, for the sake of only 30p, why would you deny yourself the opportunity of owning the car of your dreams?"

The customer bought the car when the price difference was put into a different context. It's possible that the arithmetic will hurt the customer's brain, as well, as evidenced by the scribbles on the sheet of paper left behind after the customer left the dealer-ship in his new car. (So have a calculator to hand.)

So the purpose of the Reduce It To The Ridiculous Close is to put the price difference into another context, and to change the customer's mindset when considering any price objection. The basic rule in this close is that the customer must do the arith-metic, be bogged down with the minutia of it all and in so doing, will have no choice but to realise how silly his or her objection is.

## So to summarize:

Reduce any impasse on price to the lowest amount possible denomination but include the customer in the process by making them responsible for the arithmetic.

## Seconds Out...

**The Reduce it to the Ridiculous Close** – Finding the lowest denomination.

I can use the Reduce it to the Ridiculous Close when I......

# The Tie Down Close
## These are Really Powerful, Aren't They?

This is without doubt my favourite closing technique and the best advice that I can give you is to make tie downs part of your every day voice pattern.

Those of you who subscribed to our powerful Language of Influence DVD programme series, may recognise this technique under the title of Tag Questions. Of all the closing techniques covered in this series, this one is by far the most powerful.

If you ever have the opportunity to watch a champion salesperson at work, you will notice that customers are continually nodding their head in agreement. Well, here is how you can get your customers doing the same.

First of all, never make a statement without it being for the purpose of paving the way for a question. You do this by using tie downs.

What are tie downs? They are just as they appear to be. Imagine a tent that isn't securely fastened. It can blow away, can't it? Did that make you nod? That's a tie down. They are simple phrases that end with a question mark and your customer nodding in agreement, such as:

- Isn't it?
- Couldn't you?
- Wouldn't it?
- Aren't you?
- Don't you?

If you put one of these tie downs on the end of any statement, you will turn it into a very powerful closing question, wont you?

And, if you can make eye contact and nod your head at the same time, people will almost find it impossible to resist, won't they? Seeing you nod your head in agreement, in conjunction with using a tie down will cause the reaction you want, won't it?

Whenever I am with someone and I want him or her to agree with me, all I have to do is use a tie down, isn't it?

### So to summarize:

Tie downs, like pegs in your tent guy ropes, make your sale more stable....don't they?

**The Tie Down Close** – Isn't it? Doesn't it? Wont they...?

I can use the Tie Down Close when I......

# The Summary Question Close
## I Want to Think About it!

How do you feel when the customer says, "I want to think about it"?

Too often salespeople just accept this as the one question that cannot be answered. Others dive in and ask, "What do you want to think about?"

The customer replies with the predictable answer, "Everything really."

Before we analyse how the summary question close works, let's take a look at how it arises in the first place, so we can possibly avoid it from occurring to you.

What does it really mean when the customer says he or she wants to think about it?

Usually, it means that they have run out of objections and cannot think of any other way of saying, no to you. In other words, they want to buy, but would also like some breathing space.

Every good salesperson knows that giving customers too much space gives another salesperson a chance to steal the sale.

That in mind, staying true to the rule of having empathy with the customer and also making him or her feel comfortable, we need some way of closing them without violating their need for space.

The summary question close is just the close we need in this instance.

The first thing we need to do is to get the customer to relax, and we can do that by expressing empathy that he wants to, "Think about it." We can achieve this by responding, "Of course you do, and if I were in your position, I would want to think about it too."

Now, this leads the customer into a nice relaxed frame of mind because now he thinks that you are going to let him go.

Instead, without hesitation, you follow up with, "But, whilst we are together, what was it you wanted to think about, was it the delivery date?"

It is important here that we choose a really safe part of the sales presentation that has already been agreed upon. The customer then answers in the negative, "No, it's not the delivery date." This of course is a positive step, because he or she has now agreed with the delivery date.

You then follow-up with another safe option, "Was it the fact that we agreed on the King Size?"

Again, the customer answers with a negative, which actually confirms his positive position.

By listing all the things that you have already agreed, you are creating double negatives, thereby creating a positive.

The one thing you purposely omit is price, because this would just be an invitation to introduce a discount.

As the customer agrees to each point, he or she now begins to realise that the tactic of, wanting to think about it, is getting weaker with each objection removed.

This then forces out the real one, which is usually a price or specification issue.

This could be a condition or an objection - a condition being something beyond your control, and an objection being something you haven't explained properly.

If you can satisfy the condition or overcome the objection you can now close the sale.

---

**Three important points to remember when using the Summary Question Close are:**

1. Do not pause when you ask, "What was it you wanted to think about?" In other words, go straight into your first point.

2. Do not mention price

3. Give the customer the space he or she needs with, "Of course you do, and if I were you, I would want to think about it too."

---

## So to summarize:

When people say They want to think about it, use the Summary Question close to find out exactly what they want to think about.

**The Summary Question Close** – What exactly is it you want to think about? Is it......?

I can use the Summary Question Close when I......

## The Similar Situation Close
### I've Seen it All Before

This is another great close for those customers who just cannot make up their mind.

The similar situation close is one that can be used in any industry or profession, but is especially powerful in the service sector where you'll find some kind of misfortune that may befall the customer if they don't invest.

Examples of these are:

- The insurance business
- Tax investigations
- Product warranties

There are many stories of insurance salespeople, who in trying to sell a policy, will paint terrible pictures of accidents and how they would leave a family in dire straits if the customer were to not go ahead and purchase a policy.

The salesperson goes on to outline all the misfortunes that could happen and the terrible consequences that may result, only to finish with the immortal line. "And we wouldn't want that to happen to you, would we?"

How far you take this is entirely a matter for your own conscience to determine.

However, I recently had the pleasure of working with a truly professional salesperson who was selling insurance in the East of the UK. The particular product he was selling was for flood damage.

This fellow had researched his product and market quite well and as part of his sales presentation, he outlined the fact that the customer's house was built on a "flood plain".

He had taken the time to research not only the location of the house but also had the statistics for the damage caused to houses for various levels of flood within the vicinity of this customer's home.

As he was summing up his presentation, he told the story of a young couple in a similar situation to his customer's, to whom he had presented the previous year without success.

He shared with this customer how badly he had felt when they had been caught in the recent flooding. He ended his presentation with, "And we wouldn't want that to happen to you would we?"

The couple bought a policy and are now adequately protected against future floods.

That is how the similar situation works.

## So to summarize:

Look for a scenario where you have presented a similar product or service with a negative outcome. Introduce it with the phrase, "This reminds me of a similar situation." Then outline your comparison. When you have finished, say to the customer, "And we wouldn't want that to happen to you would we?"

## Seconds Out...

**The Similar Situation Close** – Using your previous experience to get a "No" to a "Yes!"

I can use the Similar Situation Close when I......

# The Unfair Question Close
## When a Definite No! Equals a Yes!

This is a fantastic close to use when you have a unique or obvious benefit for the customer.

To explain how it works, allow me to tell you a story about a young man who had the misfortune to find himself in the dock in a court of law.

I don't know whether you have taken notice of this, but barristers and attorneys always ask closed questions. This is by no means a coincidence, but a technique they all learn. (Questions that only invite a Yes or a No response).

This allows them to frame the answer in their client's favour.

Well, this particular young man kept answering questions with questions, despite being repeatedly warned by the judge that he should answer the question as he'd been asked, with a simple declarative statement, Yes or No!

Finally, the judge, losing his patience, said that if the young man persisted, he would find him in contempt of court and punish him with a custodial sentence.

The young man looked at the judge quizzically and said he would be happy to comply, on one condition.

The judge, looking for an amicable resolution to the problem in hope of moving on with the trial, asked what that condition might be.

"Well", said the young man, "Would you answer just one question for me, with a yes or no?"

Wanting to finally put an end to matters the judge agreed.

"OK," said the young man, "Do you still beat your wife as hard as you used to?"

Now that is an unfair question! How could the judge answer?

If the judge responds, "No!", this opens the door for the man in the dock to respond:

"Oh so what? Do you beat her harder or softer? But, you do still beat her!"

Or, assuming that he can somehow get out of this foolishness, he can respond, "Yes!", but he'll regret it even more!

"And does she enjoy the consistency of a regular beating?"

So, an unfair question is one that makes the wrong answer difficult.

I know our marketing department use this one all the time. "Why would you refuse yourself and your company the opportunity of hearing, in a no obligation half-hour meeting? How we can improve the results of your business?"

The standard answer we receive is, "Well, I wouldn't."

We then use the assumptive close and the alternative close in combination with the unfair question to make the appointment.

These are very powerful ways of getting customers to really think.

## So to summarize:

Ask your question in a way that leaves your customer with no choice but to agree with you! Unfair isn't it? (Was that a Tie Down as well?)

## Seconds Out...

**The Unfair Question Close** – Why would you refuse.....?

I can use the Unfair Question Close when I......

# The Shut Up Close
## The First One to Speak Loses

I guess technically you could argue that this isn't really a close,

After all, to successfully implement it, it requires you to do and say nothing.

However, if you learn nothing else from this book, this is vital – you must learn when to shut up. (God gave us two ears and only one mouth – he must have been trying to tell us something! Use them in that proportion.)

Whenever you ask the customer a question, just shut up and give him or her a chance to answer.

This is true of any question, but especially appropriate in a potential sales situation.

Quite frankly, there are few things more infuriating than a sales person who is on a roll and won't stop for breath or actually listen to his customer.

Silence brings enormous pressure to bear and is a fabulous weapon for the sales champion in forcing the customer to commit to an answer.

**In fact, the golden rule is; "the first person to speak loses."**

This reminds me of an experience I had when buying some home office furniture.

The sales consultant had done a great job in designing some office space under the stairs in my house and I had indicated my desire to go ahead, if we could agree on the price.

After some negotiation, we found we were slightly apart on price, and after much "gnashing" of his calculator the sales consultant told me he had gone as far as he could.

I smiled, thanked him for all his effort, complimented him on his design, and showed empathy for his position.

Then I asked him to consider splitting the difference with me, in other words, go halves with me on the price difference.

He looked at me and I looked at him, it was like a wild west stand off between two gunslingers.

This guy was well trained, I can tell you that. The silence that ensued went on and on until I got a bit fed up and started to read the evening paper.

At this point my wife came into the room and looking somewhat perplexed, she noticed me reading the paper and looked over at this complete stranger, who was just staring in my direction.

The quizzical look on her face produced a reaction from the sales consultant.

He looked at her and said, "I know what he is doing, the first one to speak loses."

Oops! He lost, we made the compromise.

## So to summarize:

The power of silence. Ask a closing question and then shut up!

## Seconds Out...

**The Shut up Close** – Silence brings its own pressure.

I can use the Shut up Close when I......

# The "Is it Me?" Close
## Confidence Minus Ego = A Win/Win Situation

In my experience, at one time or another as a salesperson you must be prepared to put your ego on hold. If you are to become sales champions, it won't happen any other way.

While it is indeed necessary to call upon your confidence to be successful, I recommend that you position yourself just south of arrogance and just north of confidence and at no time should a customer feel as if you are superior to him or her.

In fact, one of the rules I live by is "the art of diplomacy is letting the other person have your own way." Remember earlier we spoke about having the customer feel empowered to make the decision to buy from you rather than his feeling he was sold something? To implement the Is it Me close, takes a certain amount of courage because of the answers that could potentially arise as a result of such introspection. Regardless what comes out of this questioning, you need to be in control of your ego at all times.

Using this style of closing, it draws out the real objections from the potential customer. As such, it should only be used at the very end of the sale after you have tried everything else you've learned. In other words, you've assumed the sale is yours, you've done the balance sheet, and the Trial close and your customer is just not budging. We can only conclude one thing – it's you and I realize this is tough to hear and this why it is imperative that you again, "leave your ego at the door" before you go down this road.

To deliver this close, my advice is that you put the customer at ease first with a statement such as the following:

"Despite my best efforts to outline the benefits, I can see that you are still having difficulty making your decision. May I ask you a question?"

Wait for the customer to answer. This allows him to feel even more at ease.

"Is it me?" When you ask, look him straight in the eyes. This conveys confidence and your genuine desire to get to the bottom of this.

This of course falls into the category of a question, one that you can anticipate what the answers may be; although one of them might not be what you are hoping for.

I found that this question is often followed by a spluttering, "No, no, not at all it's just that..."'

From there, you usually learn what the real objection is, which is normally price, specification or timing. In other words something you can easily overcome, move on and close the sale.

But, what if he says, "Yes, actually it is you!"

Well, take a deep breath, swallow your pride, and refer back to the ego discussion. Think not about you and your ego but about your company and being able to salvage the sale, even if means that you will lose the commission. Think of the bigger picture, please.

And remember that the art of diplomacy is letting the other person have your own way. Look suitably hurt and then say, "And, is that the only thing stopping you from going ahead?"

If the answer is yes, offer to introduce someone else from your organisation to complete the sale. This will accomplish two things. It will save the sale, but at the same time, it removes any discomfort of the customer having to disclose his feelings.

The fact that you were savvy enough to pick up on this without his having to spell it out will prove to be far more positive than you'll ever know. In fact, he may, as a result of your intuition, end up referring you and your company to a colleague or a friend.

The last bit of advice I have in this category is, don't let it ruin your day, as the saying goes: "You can't please all the people, all of the time."

### So to summarize:

The golden rule is; "the art of diplomacy is letting the other person have your own way."

## Seconds Out...

**The "Is it Me?" Close** – A straight forward way to remove the final barrier.

I can use the "Is it Me?" Close when I......

# At a Glance Guide
## To all the Closes we've covered

**The Direct Close:** A Direct Question asking for commitment.

**The Alternative Close:** Always look to give your customer a choice by using questions which end with an alternative.

**The Assumptive Close**: Never ask permission, always assume the positive....

**The Decisional Close:** If the customer asks you for any kind of commitment, return the request...

**The Sharp Angle Close:** Is ideal for getting the customer into the 'yes' mode – "was it ..... you really wanted?"

**The Trial Close:** Gentle questions that give the customer a safe place to say 'no' without jeopardising the sale.

**The Puppy Dog Close:** Let people try your product or service - set up a trial period, lend it to them... etc.

**The Balance Sheet Close:** Confirm all the positives on your side and then let the customer come up with the negatives.

**The Lost Sale Close:** Is when you are face to face and the customer says *"No!"*

**The Subject to Close:** Is perfect when the customer says I need to talk to my....(third party).

**The Major/ Minor Close:** Is a technique for asking the customer for commitment without using the words and focusing on a lesser choice (which pen to use).

**The Final Objection Close:** Is a great way to avoid answering objection after objection - *"is that the only thing stopping us from going ahead?"*

**The Hope and Fear Close:** Make sure all concessions are time bound.

**The Reduce it to the Ridiculous Close:** Finding the lowest denomination.

**The Tie Down Close:** Isn't it? Doesn't it? Wont they...?

**The Summary Question Close:** What exactly is it you want to think about? Is it......?

**The Similar Situation Close:** Using your previous experience to get a "No" to a "Yes!"

**The Unfair Question Close:** Why would you refuse.....?

**The Shut up Close:** Silence brings its own pressure.

**The "Is it Me " Close:** A straight forward way to remove the final barrier.

# Bonus
# Section

# The Secret 5 Step Formula-Overcomes Every Objection

# The Secret 5 Step Formula...Overcomes Every Objection

Objections are the life blood of all good salespeople. Often when working with salespeople they bemoan the fact that customers raise objections. Sometimes, even with the intonation that the customers have no right to even think about objections.

But, let us put this into context. Firstly, objections only arise because people have a genuine desire to buy your product or service and, they need your help to clarify any sticking points in their own mind, and as any good marketer knows that is where the battle for the customers business really takes place, in the customers mind!

Secondly, most objections arise because of poor qualification skills, or a badly planned sales pitch on behalf of the sales person. Think about it, if the customer has some questions then there is obviously something that hasn't been covered to their satisfaction, some information that is missing. In other words you haven't established what is important to the customer in the first place, or your sales pitch doesn't present the right information in the right order.

Of course just taking this line is unfair on you. The customer might think of questions as we go through the sales process, something might become apparent that they hadn't thought of before. This of course may mean that you the salesperson created the objection in the first place, so be careful what you say and how you say it!

The reality however, is that objections arise for a number of reasons and there are some really effective techniques that you can use to minimise the impact and help customers become ready to buy.

Some customers arrive at the beginning of your sales process with a list of questions, these are the things that should be uncovered during the 'discovery' phase of your sales process, and with skill and practice these are the easier objections to overcome, others that arise during the process should, with practice, become easy to anticipate and therefore easy to deal with and provide the right answers.

Every industry and product has its own unique set of objections, and indeed it is often argued that every customer is different and therefore it is almost impossible to anticipate their objections and be ready for them.

This however, is not something to which I would subscribe; the human species is in fact very predictable in its behaviour. There are numerous examples of how people respond predictably to a simple stimulus.

Try this, next time you are walking down the street with your friend, both of you stop and look up and point. I guarantee that within a few minutes you will have a small group of people looking up into the sky with you, a predictable result!

Or, as you walk down the high street try smiling at everyone, make eye contact if you can (although this isn't absolutely necessary because people will see you in their peripheral vision and smile.) and notice how many people smile back – a predictable response.

Let us not be too literal here, the cynics  amongst you who try this  will say that not everyone smiled, well I am prepared to bet that at least 98% did, it's a predictable response. Try yawning in the company of other people and see what happens. (Especially the cynics.)

In exactly the same way, if you say the same things to the same type of people in the same way, you are very likely to get the same response. Remember earlier we talked about only asking questions to which you already know the answer; well this is another example of how you can put yourself in the driving seat when dealing with customers.

Let us also deal with the idea that all customers are different. This is only marginally true. Firstly, there is a limited number of behaviour and communication preferences as defined by eminent psychologists such as C.G.Jung (and ancient Greek philosophers like Heraclitus) plus, by definition, the people you deal with pre-qualify themselves by the very fact that they have presented themselves as customers for your product or service.

Every product and service provides a potential benefit for the customer. If your product or service does not provide that benefit then you are sat in front of the wrong customer.

There are also a number of truisms to bear in mind when thinking of why people don't buy; no need, no want or, no money / budget, and if any of these are true then again you are sitting in front of the wrong customer.

In retailing, I often use the phrase, "they are not here to tell you that they don't want one." So for example, if you are selling cars, then it would be strange for someone to wake up one morning and think 'I am going to change my car today,' drive into town and pop in to the local Car dealership and say 'I just thought, out of courtesy, I would pop in and let you know, that although I am changing my car I won't be buying it from you.'

Therefore, the only reason for being there is to let the car salesperson have the opportunity to help them reach a buying decision. Whether that is positive in favour of the salesperson or not may rest entirely on their skill as a salesperson.

By the same token, if you are in 'Business to Business' sales and you find yourself talking with someone who has no genuine desire or need for your product then you are certainly making life difficult by going to see them or calling them.

When prospecting, you should have the simple goal of finding people who have a genuine (even if it is tentative) acceptance that at some point they are prepared to consider the product or service for sale. The specifics around timing and/or desire, will define the time and effort that you are prepared to invest and the level of objection that you will receive.

As a consequence of the above I am going to assume that your selection of customer has been excellent, and you have in front of you (or you are going through the sales process with) someone who has a real need or desire to work with you to help them through the buying process.

In this scenario you should welcome objections as they are buying signals, and answering them effectively will move the sale forwards.

Twenty years ago I was employed as a Trainee Consultant for an established consultancy business, and part of my responsibility was to generate sales leads. At that time I didn't have any experience of selling training or consultancy programmes. I read a book by an American Real Estate salesman, Mark McCormack which suggested that salespeople should keep a log of all objections which stop them from gaining a sale. Thinking this to be good advice I bought myself a small notebook.

Each time I had difficulty with a sale, I would make a note of the objection on the left hand page, then after having given things some thought, I would write the answer, or answers if I could think of more than one, on the right hand side. This would then allow me time to give some real thought to my answers, and learn from each sales pitch.

For more common objections I decided the best strategy was to build the answer into the sales presentation, which stopped them coming up in the first place.
This worked particularly well for a Motor Manufacturer I did

some work with. They had a reputation for rust, and quite a number of customers mentioned it, but they had solved the issue and were now offering an extended warranty because they were so confident of the answer.

My advice was to put their biggest objection up front and start all their presentations with the statement "some people think that our product rusts" if the customer answered "yeah I heard that" then the salesperson would say "well, you know we solved this and now we offer an extended 10 year warranty on the body-work, to satisfy your concerns and display our confidence in the actions we have taken" followed by the confirmation question "I'm sure like all our happy customers that will satisfy your concerns over rust won't it?"

If the customer had said "oh, I hadn't heard that" the salesperson would say "oh yes but we've solved that issue now and we offer the longest warranty in the automotive business on our bodywork" followed by the confirmation question "so it needn't be a concern need it?"

However, the biggest lesson that I learned was that most of the objections (and I genuinely thought that there were a lot of them) were a variation on a theme. There were in fact only five major objections to selling consultancy.

This knowledge allowed me to go on and sell millions of pounds worth of consultancy programmes.

This one piece of knowledge has also been responsible for the success of hundreds of salespeople I have had the privilege of working with over the last twenty years.

The real success of the "Objection Journal" is in the fact that it forces you to review each sales pitch you make, and analyse what worked and what didn't. Furthermore it provides an opportunity to learn from your own mistakes.

But more importantly it allows you time to craft the perfect answer.

Think of it like this, sometimes when you are at a party or maybe even having a disagreement with someone and they say something, and you can't think of a clever answer. However, the next day after letting your unconscious mind work on it, you think of the perfect answer. Often followed by the statement – "I wish I'd thought of that yesterday! The next time that happens,  I'm going to say ..."

But of course you forget. Well, the "Objections Journal" can make sure you remember. By writing the objections on the left hand page and the ideal answers on the right hand page, you have the opportunity to review every objection you have received before every sales presentation.

It doesn't take long for you to become familiar with your common objections and you begin to relax in your presentations, focus on your customer and even welcome the objections because you now know you have the answer and every time you answer an objection it takes you closer to the order.

In conclusion, learn to love objections; they are the lifeblood of champion salespeople!

When you have established your key objections there are five golden rules to follow which will help you deal with them effectively but, just before we move on to identifying what they are, there is one final point I would like to make.

Some objections are not just features and benefits on which customers may like clarification, some may be described as 'conditions.'

A condition could be described as a physical property which makes the product or service inappropriate to your customers needs.

For example, a one bedroom apartment would not be suitable for a family of six with children ranging in age from 4 to 18 years old. A small two seater sports car would not suit a family of four who go on regular picnics and camping holidays.

A condition may also be something that is entirely outside the customers budget. So typically a condition is not something that the salesperson can overcome with explanations of features and benefits. Usually a condition is a deal breaker, and it is better for the salesperson to move on to the next sale.

However, for those that fall outside the criteria of condition, the following rules will prove very helpful in persuading others to your point of view.

# STEP No. 1 – Ignore it / by - pass it

This may seem a strange piece of advice in a world where we are all educated that the customer is always King. So, let me explain; Sometimes customers will offer objections as a way of interacting in the sales process. The objection may not be real; it may just be an attempt at a clever (or not so clever) interjection.

The danger with attempting to answer an objection at the first hearing is that you legitimise it, you give it some energy and the risk is that you turn it into a REAL objection.

Much better to take the politicians way out, acknowledge the comment and move on to something else. Don't worry, this isn't rude or ignorant. Plus, I would never advise you to do anything that would harm your chances of getting the sale.

The way politicians handle difficult questions from political commentators can provide us with some fantastic pointers in acknowledging a question and moving on.

For example, if the political interviewer were to ask a question which the politician did not want to answer they might say something like "that's a very interesting question, but let me answer this one first..."

In a sales situation when the customer brings up an objection, particularly early on in the process, a good way of deflecting it without rudely ignoring the customer could be;

"I understand your concern and will come back to that later, by the way, one of the major benefits of owning/using our... product and/or service..." ('by the way'....changes the direction of the conversation - and it is something people do all the time, without realising. Try it, it works a treat!)

This allows you to move on having acknowledged the prospects question. If the objection is a real objection then it will definitely raise its ugly head again very soon, or as a final objection at the end of your pitch.

So, you must avoid being put into the situation where you get dragged into answering question after question after question.

Now, clearly there will be some consistent questions that the majority of prospects are likely to ask. As you are a professional salesperson I am going to assume that you know what these questions are ( and if you don't then I suggest you monitor future presentations and identify them) and that you have built your sales presentation to deal with them as you move through the 'pitch.'

When a question raises its head out of sequence then you are definitely entitled to advise the prospect that you will deal with his/her concerns later. In situations where the question isn't dealt with within the 'pitch' then you need to find out how serious the prospect really is about the objection.

Clearly we can't just ask 'do you really mean that? So the best way for us to test it is to just by-pass it and see if it comes up again. In summary – rule number one is ('by the way'...) 'ignore it/by-pass it' and see if it comes up again, or if you get any resistance to this then it is real, if the prospect brings it up again later on, it is real.

# STEP No. 2 – Clarify it!

This is important too! Do not attempt to answer an objection until you have clarified exactly what the objection is and why the prospect thinks it is a barrier to the sale.

The danger is you often make assumptions about what the customer is about to say, has just said or was going to say. Usually these assumptions are based on previous experience of different prospects and what they have said in the past.

Remember the psychology of the sales environment is that you should always have more people saying no to you than saying yes. (If that isn't the case then you are playing too safe and not talking to, or asking, enough people for their business.)

This means that you are getting regular feedback as to why people don't want to buy. Because of this, it is important that you keep things in context. It becomes very easy for the standard reasons people give for not buying to become standard excuses for why you can't sell.

So, when you think that an objection is real, paraphrase it back to the customer with a phrase such as "just so that I understand what you are saying ..." And then paraphrase your understanding of the objection.

This then confirms your understanding of the customer concern is what they mean. For example, if a customer says your product or service is "too expensive..." what do they mean?

Do they mean "I cannot afford it"? Or "it is beyond my budget"? Or "it is more expensive than an alternative that I have seen"? Any one of these could mean "it is too expensive." So the key question here could be "may I just clarify what you mean when you say too expensive? Compared to what?"

# STEP No.3 – Isolate it

The danger of being a salesperson who is customer centric (not that you shouldn't be, but there are dangers.) Is that you feel the need to answer every prospect objection. The risk here is that after you have answered one objection, the prospect comes up with another, then another, then another and so on...

Your sales presentation then becomes an objection answering session. In order to avoid this, be certain that you are answering a genuine objection, be sure you understand it fully and then make sure you understand where it sits in the prospect's hierarchy of needs.

What, I here you ask, is the prospects hierarchy of needs? Let me explain. Prospects who are serious about purchasing a product or service will have a series of questions in their own mind about various aspects of the features and benefits of your product/service.

They will obviously have in their mind, things like; specification requirements, delivery dates, colours, price guidelines, etc. Each one of these needs will be in a particular hierarchical order, in other words, one will be more important than another.

Because of this, it is vital that you understand your customers and their buying motives; this will allow you to build your sales presentation to answer anticipated customer questions.

Therefore, when you get an objection, you can defer answering it until later in the presentation, if you know the answer is coming up, or choose to answer it immediately.

However, my best advice is find out what else is on the prospect's mind by asking, "And is that the only thing stopping you from going ahead?"

# The Secret 5 Step Formula... Overcomes Every Objection

From our earlier text you will remember we should never ask a question unless we can anticipate the answer.

One answer might be, "Yes" which would mean that if you answer the objection you have made a sale!

If the answer is "No" then you would be entitled to ask "what else is on your mind at this point?" The answer to this will tell you how much work you have to do before convincing the prospect to go ahead and purchase.

At this juncture you have a couple of options

    a) If the answer to most of the customer queries are dealt with in what is left of your presentation, you can inform the prospect you will be covering his/her key concerns during the rest of your presentation.

    b) If the concerns arise towards the end of your presentation and are not going to be covered, start answering them in order of the easiest first, this way if there are any questions which you cannot satisfy you can 'surround and outweigh' the concern with your other answers. (I will show you how later in the book)

The most important thing is to understand exactly what the objection is and what answering it means to you and to the customer.

# STEP No. 4 – If necessary answer it!

There are a number of options for answering prospect objections

→  Boast about it
→  Feed it back
→  Change the base
→  Put them in your shoes
→  Reduce it to the ridiculous
→  Compare it
→  Surround and outweigh

**Boast about it...**
The first one in the list may be the biggest surprise for many people, but it is a very effective way of answering regular  objections I was commissioned a few years ago to run a project for an automotive manufacturer, who for a number of years had suffered a reputation of selling cars that rust. The reality was, from an engineering point of view the cars lasted up to an average of 15 years, and therefore were seen on the roads in states of disrepair more often than others because they were mechanically better

As part of the sales process I advised salespeople to boast about the reputation for rust, and then answer with the measures taken by the manufacturer to combat any rust problems and outline the 10 year paint warranty.

The opening line of the sales presentation went something like "I am really pleased that you have decided to look at owning a xyz car. Many people think that xyz cars rust.  However, we now offer a 10 year guarantee for the bodywork, how long do you usually keep your cars before you change for a new one? (The answer was usually 2 or 3 years)

This dealt with the objection, and answered it right at the beginning of the presentation. Taking the stress away from the salesperson, who would be anticipating the objection, and also answering the biggest question on the customers' mind, so allowing them to relax and get into the rest of the presentation.

So, think about your sales presentations over the last few months and identify your biggest and most common objection. Consider opening your presentation with "Many people think..." and the providing the answer.

Just be sure that you understand the objection, it is genuine and be clear that this is the right strategy for your product or service (try it a couple of times and judge the reaction from the customer)

**Feed it back...**
This is a good way to make prospects justify their own objection and in many cases when you do this they will realise just how minor or futile the objection really is, at worst it will give you more information about the specifics that surround the objection.

Let us take the 'too expensive' example. If a customer says 'it is too expensive' you should adopt a quizzical air and 'feedback' the objection to the customer, by asking "too expensive?"

If the customer has a problem with the delivery schedule, the salesperson could ask "the delivery schedule?"

Typically the customer will then justify their objection, either talking themselves out of it, or providing further information so giving the salesperson an opening to find an acceptable solution.

**Change the base...**
This particular technique requires that the salesperson be skilled at changing the direction of the conversation.

> **Two key phrases come to mind for this to be made easy;**
>
> *"by the way..."*
> *"incidentally..."*

Changing the base of the objection requires that the salesperson re-direct the customer's attention to a more value added feature of the product/service.

If the customer mentions the price as in "it's too expensive..." the salesperson may respond with "I understand your initial concerns. Incidentally, did I mention, the whole life running costs?"

Or perhaps some level of specification doesn't immediately seem to suit the customer, this could be swapped for some other benefit or feature with the response "that's a good point, by the way we haven't covered how this works when we....."

'Changing the Base' is a technique which ensures that you manage to get your number one benefit across to the customer and you can use your customers objection as springboard to a positive presentation of other features and benefits.

**Put them in your shoes...**
Putting the customer in your shoes is a sensible technique to create a better understanding of the objection from your perspective.

# The Secret 5 Step Formula... Overcomes Every Objection

So let us once again take the obvious example of price. Should the customer bring up the age old issue of "It is too expensive..." the salesperson may answer...

"You are not the first person to say that to me. Let me ask you, if you were in my shoes what would you do?"

This may prompt the answer "I would reduce the price" to which a sensible answer might be "and if I weren't able to do that, but really wanted your business, what else would you suggest?"

The answer to this question will always take you closer to the sale. On a different tack, during the project I mentioned earlier for automative manufacturer we also offered this technique for dealing with the rust objection.

When a prospect mentioned the rust issue, the suggested response was "let me ask you a question? If you had a product that had a reputation for rust, what would you do about it?"

Of course the standard answer was "well I would get it sorted!" To which we suggested the salesperson answer "that's exactly what we have done. We now offer a 10 year guarantee on the paint work."

Putting the customer in your shoes gives you direct access to how they would sell to themselves.


## Reduce it to the ridiculous...
This technique deals with money and time. If for example, you are say £300 apart on the price of something the prospect would keep for three years, the conversation might proceed along the lines of ...

Salesperson: "Well Mr/Mrs customer may I ask how long you are

likely to keep the ...?"
Customer: "About three years"
Salesperson: "Fine, so that would be how much per year?"
Customer: "£100"
Salesperson: "And how often will you use the...?"
Customer: "Every day"
Salesperson: "So on a weekly basis that would be about...?"
Customer: "£2"
Salesperson: "And you said you would use it everyday, how much does that work out to daily?"
Customer: "About 70p I guess"
Salesperson: "So you are saying, for the sake of only 70p per day you are prepared to deny yourself the opportunity to .."

---

**There are however some golden rules with this one:**

*Firstly*, the customer must do the arithmetic, and if the sums are complex make sure you have a calculator to hand.

*Secondly*, there must be a clear rationale for the process.

*And thirdly*, if at the end you want to compare the amount to something trivial like a newspaper or packet of cigarettes, make sure you know the customer well enough to choose the right product. Cigarettes won't be a valid comparison for non-smokers

---

**Compare it...**
This is similar to changing the base, except that rather than redirect the customers' attention we are overtly going to compare their concern to another feature/benefit.

So sticking with the price example "it's too expensive..."

Salesperson could say: "I understand your concern on the level of investment required, however when you compare it to the fact that we have included the ... and the... plus you get the bonus of having...etc."

Or maybe the colour is a problem.

The salesperson may say something along the lines of "I know you are disappointed that we cannot get you the exact colour, but is that the most important thing when compared to our speed of delivery?"

**Surround and Outweigh...**
This final section on answering objections has already been alluded to earlier. This is where we take the customer's objection and we surround and outweigh it with all the other features and benefits associated with purchasing the product or service you sell - very similar to the Balance Sheet close.

"So Mr/Mrs customer, recognise we can't get you the exact colour match, we are in a position to get you a, b, c, d, e and f which were really important to you, weren't they?" (Tie Down close.) Emphasise the positive, to eliminate the negative.

# STEP No 5 – Confirm it

Never ever assume that just because you have become adept at using these techniques and you have followed the five golden rules, that the customer has had his objection satisfactorily answered.

The only way you can be absolutely sure is to ask the question. So, whichever technique you choose, always finish by being assumptive and confirming the customers' agreement that you have answered any query or objection to their absolute satisfaction.

A suggested closing question might be "so I guess that clears that up then doesn't it?" Or

"Before we move on, may I confirm that I have answered your concerns to your complete satisfaction?"

# Conclusion

Overcoming objections, like closing the sale or negotiation techniques, offers no guarantees that you will get every sale for which you pitch.

What I can guarantee is that it will improve how you handle objections and will avoid those awkward silences, when neither you nor the customer knows what to say next.

Utilizing these techniques will also help you relax during your presentation because you will have the weapons in your armoury to handle any objection from price, to colour to delivery. Whatever the objection you now have everything you need to make a positive step towards closing the sale.

Customers will also appreciate your professionalism in handling their questions, and how you provide an environment whereby they can articulate their concerns and your ability to put their mind at rest.

This Secret 5 Step Formula for overcoming every objection can and will revolutionise the way you handle objections in the future.

# Your
# Objection Journal

In the Objection section I mention the dramatic effect an "Objection Journal" had on my sales, so I thought - "Let's provide one for you!"

On the following pages you can write your unanswered objection or sticking point in the left had page. And when you have thought of the appropriate    response(s) you can write them on the right hand page.

Regularly review your journal (before every pitch) and you will soon be answering every objection easily.

Good Luck, and Good Selling!

Rob

## Journal

OBJECTION

## Journal

ANSWER

**Journal**

OBJECTION

**Journal**

ANSWER

# I have produced an *amazing* set of DVD's and a superb programme of Audio Cd's for you to access.

The key to success with the *'Ultimate Knockout Closing System'* is learning as many techniques as possible and then how to put them into combinations. This unique set of DVD's and Audio Cd's will help you learn and understand all the 20 Heavyweight techniques and you will quickly get to grips with putting them together to create your very own bespoke *'Ultimate Knockout Closing System'* and developing some amazing closing combinations.

Simply visit www.RobPurfield.com/ukcsBoxset for more information about this programme.

## ATTEND A PRIVATE LIVE SEMINAR

..... AND SAVE £200 on the normal price! Apply NOW for your place on an exclusive *"SELLMORE PROFIT CLINIC"*

Throughout the year I run a number of 'Closed Door' *SELLMORE PROFIT CLINICS* for the people who buy my products and other special guests. If you are a high performer who qualifies to participate, I will take you through an exhilarating makeover of your selling style, and share in person some amazing sales strategies to REVOLUTIONISE YOUR SALES PROCESS.

*The SELLMORE PROFIT CLINICS are the ultimate solution for any sales professional wanting up to the minute information on persuasion and influence.*

**What you will learn:**
- Real working techniques
- Strategies, specially designed to turn enquiries into sales
- Learn the 7 **biggest secrets** of the worlds number one salesperson
- Strategies which will DOUBLE YOUR SALES IN JUST ONE YEAR!

Telephone +44(0)1482 661177 for more information
Visit www.SellMoreClinic.com

Here are just a few comments from some of my past seminars;

*"The session Rob delivered was a very positive experience for everyone. To sum it up I would say it was 'real'. This guy was not reading off a script. He clearly understands us and he understands sales. The process he taught us really does work. We have sold extra cars and the handwritten letters have also had a positive impact on our CSS scores. We are now No. 1 in our zone for customer satisfaction. I would 100% recommend this training to all other sales professionals"*
**Javed Sultan Sales Manager UK**

*"There are not many courses of this calibre about for experienced sellers and I loved the way it was delivered. Rob treats his audience with respect. My guys came away buzzing. It enlightened us all and we have completely bought into it. It was well put together and based on truth. I thought it was phenomenal*
**Shelia Randall – Toyota Sheffield**

*"We got a huge amount from this course and because we have embraced the formula 100%, it's working beautifully for us.*
**Phil Openshaw Hull UK**

127